Watch Out Below!
3-D Battle of the Sharks

Written by Lisa Regan

Designed, Developed & Published by Red Bird Publishing Ltd., U.K.
Original 3-D special effects developed by
Red Bird Publishing Ltd., U.K.

This edition published by Scholastic Inc.,
557 Broadway, New York, NY 10012,
by arrangement with Red Bird Publishing Ltd.

COPYRIGHT © 2015 Red Bird Publishing Ltd., U.K.
www.red-bird.co.uk

10 9 8 7 6 5 4 3 2 1

SCHOLASTIC INC.

WATCH OUT BELOW!

Sharks are one of the world's oldest and most fascinating creatures. There are around 400 species. All of them eat other creatures, but not all are terrifying, flesh-devouring killers. Most are actually harmless to humans, but people still kill millions of sharks every year. Sadly, several species are in danger of becoming extinct.

Read on to find out about the world's scariest and safest species in our top ten SHARK TO SHARK encounters.

CONTENTS

SHARK ATTACK!

THE FACTS

The smallest sharks are tiny: shorter than the height of this book! Species like the pygmy shark and dwarf lanternshark only grow to around 8 in (20 cm) long. The largest species is the whale shark, reaching over 45 ft (14 m) long. All of these are completely harmless–unless you're a shrimp or plankton.

Hunters such as the great white, bull shark, and tiger shark prefer a diet of squid, turtles, and seals, so they are equipped with a mighty set of jaws and teeth. This makes them a potential danger to humans if they were to accidentally cross paths with us.

However, there are still only a small number of reported shark attacks each year, and only a few of these are fatal. You are much more likely to get struck by lightning or involved in a car accident on your way to the beach . . .

SHARK ATTACK!

1
GREAT WHITE vs WHALE SHARK

Let's take a closer look at two of the world's biggest sharks.

GREAT WHITE

The great white shark has a
bad reputation as a killer. It is
responsible for more unprovoked
attacks on people than any other
type of shark. It has razor-sharp
teeth (around 3,000 of them!) that
can easily chomp through a seal's
skin and bones in a single bite. It
is huge, reaching lengths of 20 ft
(6 m), and fast, with an impressive
sense of smell, especially if there's
blood in the water.

WHALE SHARK

Meet the biggest shark of them all: the whale shark. It's an enormous but gentle creature that feeds on tiny plankton and small fish. It doesn't need super sharp shark teeth; it simply cruises through the water with its mouth open, collecting snacks along the way. It grows to 45 ft (14 m) long, but is so docile that divers have been known to hitch a ride on its back!

2

BASKING SHARK vs BULL SHARK

These next two sharks both swim close to land, but only one of them is a danger to people.

BASKING SHARK

If you're looking for a freaky fish, check out the basking shark! It is the second largest fish in the world (after the whale shark) and has an enormous mouth. It isn't aggressive, despite its gaping jaws. It is a filter feeder, scooping up food as it swims with its mouth open, and it can sometimes be seen at the surface feasting on crowds of plankton close to shore.

BULL SHARK

The bull shark is one of three species that is well-known for fatal attacks on humans. Not only is it large and aggressive, but it also loves shallow water. It can leave the ocean and swim into freshwater rivers, allowing it to get much closer to people than many other sharks. Experts believe this makes it the most dangerous shark species to humans.

3

TIGER SHARK vs ZEBRA SHARK

Which would you most like to meet: a tiger or a zebra?

Tiger sharks can grow as large as great whites, and they are the second-most likely species to attack humans. Scarily, they are much more likely to come back for another bite. The tiger shark is nicknamed "the garbage can of the ocean" as it will eat almost anything. They have been found with many types of animals inside their stomachs, as well as weirder items like car parts, boots, fur coats, and baseballs! Their teeth are strong and act like a can opener, allowing them to bite through tough skin and even turtle shells.

TIGER SHARK

zebra shark

This shark's name may seem odd for a spotted shark, but if you look at them when they are young you will understand why. Tiger shark babies are born with a striped pattern, which is replaced by spots as they grow bigger. Don't confuse this shark with the leopard shark, which is a different shape and size and lives in different areas. The gentle zebra shark feeds on small fish and other creatures that it sucks out of the sand.

4

BONNETHEAD vs HAMMERHEAD

Which is the most dangerous of all the hammerheads?

The bonnethead is a type of hammerhead shark, but it is the littlest and shyest and poses no threat to humans. Also called the shovelhead, it has the smallest head of all the hammerhead family. Timid and harmless, it usually sticks close to its friends in groups (called schools) of around 15 sharks. Sometimes, though, it gathers in schools of thousands to migrate to warmer water in the winter. Bonnetheads, like all hammerheads, are not well designed for floating, so they have to stay on the move or they will sink.

BONNETHEAD

The great hammerhead is a huge and impressive hunter. The unusual shape of its head may help it detect electrical signals given off by its prey. It can hunt down stingrays that are buried under the sand, and studies have even shown that these sharks can pick up the charge of a buried battery from 30 ft (9.1 m) away. Of all the hammerheads, this type is the most likely to attack humans, although no one has died from an attack.

HAMMERHEAD

5

LEOPARD SHARK vs OCEANIC WHITETIP

Meet a deep-water danger, and a shark that swims closer to home.

Leopard sharks have a beautiful pattern on their slender body. They often come close to land, swimming into bays and estuaries. They can be seen following the tide onto mudflats, looking for food like clams and crabs. However, they are not dangerous to humans at all. A leopard shark mother has lots of babies at one time: sometimes more than 30!

LEOPARD SHARK

OCeanic WHITETIP

The great diver Jacques Cousteau described the oceanic whitetip as "the world's most dangerous shark." It lives in the deep, open ocean and is known for attacking shipwrecked castaways and plane crash survivors. That makes it difficult to work out just how many people it has eaten, but it is probably more than any other shark. The oceanic whitetip is slow-moving but aggressive, and goes into a feeding frenzy when food is around, thrashing and biting anything that moves.

6

MAKO SHARK vs NURSE SHARK

One of these sharks has speed as its secret weapon . . .

The shortfin mako is the world's fastest shark, reaching speeds up to 20 mph (32 km/hr). Its name comes from the Maori word for shark. It is an aggressive hunter and has been known to attack divers and fishermen. Although it grows to 10 ft (3.2 m) long, it can make spectacular leaps right out of the water.

MAKO SHARK

NURSE SHARK

The nurse shark prefers stealth to speed and often lies in ambush on the ocean floor, waiting for its prey to swim past. Its large throat allows it to create a vacuum to suck prey into its mouth, and its skin is smooth, unlike other sharks. Nurse sharks can grow to a large size, and have strong jaws filled with thousands of tiny teeth. They are harmless to humans, unless you step on one as it lurks on the ocean floor!

7

PORT JacKson vs sand TIGER

Take a look at two toothed terrors with very distinctive features!

The Port Jackson shark is an unusual-looking fish that goes mostly unnoticed by humans. Its front and back teeth are completely different. At the front, small, sharp teeth help the shark catch fish, while the back teeth are flat and broad for cracking and crushing shellfish. Its body is an odd shape, with a blunt head, and it has black markings that look like a harness. These smaller sharks rarely grow over 3 ft (1 m) long.

PORT JACKSON

SAND TIGER

If it's sharp shark teeth you're after, look no further than the sand tiger shark. It has a mouthful of thin, pointed teeth that poke in all directions, and even show when its mouth is closed. In the wild, sand tigers live close to shore, and may attack swimmers to defend themselves. They are often seen in aquariums as they look so menacing! Their bodies are large (up to 10 ft/3 m), and the shark can alter its buoyancy by gulping mouthfuls of air.

8
REQUIEM SHARKS vs CATSHARK

Here's a contrast: a family of sleek, fast killers versus a small, harmless creature.

BLUE SHARK

Lemon Shark

Requiem sharks are fierce predators and hunt all kinds of creatures, including seabirds, octopus, fish, and mammals. The family includes lemon sharks, blue sharks, and several reef sharks, as well as bull sharks and tiger sharks. They are typically torpedo-shaped with round eyes and sharp, bladelike teeth. As a group, they are responsible for many attacks on humans.

The cute catshark is also (confusingly) known as the dogfish! It sleeps in shallow water during the day, and feeds mostly at night. Its young hatch from egg pouches that can be found on the shoreline and are nicknamed "mermaid's purses." Catsharks have extremely rough skin that can be used as a kind of sandpaper. Their skin can cause injuries if you try to grab one, but catsharks aren't a real threat to humans.

CATSHARK

9

HORN SHARK vs WOBBEGONG

These two creatures have both been known to bite humans if threatened!

HORN SHARK

The horn shark gets its name from the ridges over its eyes. It may look small and harmless, growing to about 3 ft (1 m) long, but it will bite divers if they bother it. The horn shark has powerful jaws and flat teeth for crushing shellfish, and it also has the strongest bite (for its size) of any shark. They love to eat sea urchins, and if they eat enough, their teeth turn purple!

WOBBEGONG

Watch out for the wobbegong! It may sound like a monster from a story but is in fact a "carpet shark" that lives in shallow water on the ocean floor. Its beautifully camouflaged skin is sometimes made into strong leather. Wobbegongs have been known to bite divers who touch them or swimmers who step on them: the bites are painful, and it can be hard to remove the sharks as they hang on tight. Ouch!

10

BLACKTIP SHARK VS THRESHER SHARK

Both of these sharks love to leap out of the water, but watch out for one of them!

BLACKTIP SHARK

Blacktip sharks are described as timid compared to other requiem sharks, but don't get too close! They become aggressive at feeding time and have made several attacks on swimmers. They make amazing leaps out of the water, spinning three or four times, as they feast on schools of fish.

THRESHER SHARK

The thresher shark is easily identified by its long, pointed tail. It lives away from people in the open oceans, and is shy and hard to approach. It uses its enormous tail to slap the water or swipe at and stun prey before eating it. The thresher shark has been seen leaping completely out of the water, like a dolphin.

SHARK RELATIVES

RAYS AND SKATES

Sharks are unlike most other fish: they belong to the same family as rays, and skates, called cartilaginous fish.

BLUESPOTTED STINGRAY

Instead of having a skeleton made of bones, these creatures have a substance called cartilage (like the tough bit of your nose). They don't have ribs to protect their internal organs, so they are easily crushed by their own body weight when not in water. Look out for some of them: electric rays can give a nasty shock strong enough to knock over a human, and they aren't afraid to pick a fight with divers. Stingrays have venomous stingers on their tail that can cause a painful wound or even death! Unlike rays, skates lack stingers, making them completely harmless to humans.